MIA SANCHEZ

Only you

Copyright © 2023 by Mia Sanchez

All rights reserved. No part of this publication may be reproduced, stored or transmitted in any form or by any means, electronic, mechanical, photocopying, recording, scanning, or otherwise without written permission from the publisher. It is illegal to copy this book, post it to a website, or distribute it by any other means without permission.

First edition

*This book was professionally typeset on Reedsy.
Find out more at reedsy.com*

Dedicated to the one this entire book is about...

I love you. I swear to tell you that one day.
Till then, accept my love through these poems.

Contents

Preface		iii
Acknowledgement		v
1	Society Norms	1
2	Introduction	4
3	One Sided Feelings	6
4	Dirty Little Secrets	8
5	Unspoken Confessions	10
6	Almost	12
7	These Selfish Needs of Mine	14
8	Nothing but a Stranger	17
9	Some Days	19
10	Insignificant Words	21
11	Oblivious	23
12	Patterns	26
13	Kiss Me Forever	28
14	Someone New	30
15	Fight for Me Now	32
16	Leave Me Behind	34
17	Reminisce	37
18	Distance	39
19	Everything and Nothing	41
20	Only You	43
21	An Obsession	46
22	The Beach	48

23	All I Think	50
24	Fixable	52
25	Trust Issues	54
26	One Word at a Time	56
27	Mere Words	58
28	The Future of My Dreams	60
29	A Little Broken	62
30	Be Here Tonight	64
31	Teach Me to Dream	66
32	Walk Into My Dreams	68
33	Those Moments	70
34	Beautiful Disaster	72
35	If I Fall For Someone Else	74
36	Even if I Don't Remember	76
37	One Day I Won't Walk Away	78
38	Safe and Sound	80
39	Beautiful Stranger	82
40	Always hers	84
41	Home	86
42	The Month of December	88
Also by Mia Sanchez		90

Preface

My first poetry collection "Symphony of Secrets" didn't necessarily have a proper theme.

Therefore, this time, I chose a suitable theme and attempted to write all the poems around it. Fortunately, it turned out to be easier than I had anticipated.

This collection might not contain my best poems, but, all of them are extremely special to me. Mainly, because they are about someone who I love more than anything else in this world.

My poems are in no way perfect, simply because we are all imperfect human beings. But the one who I refer to when writing them is a personification of perfection in my mind. I certainly hope that the readers will understand how much this person means to me.

I didn't want to change the initial draft just to make them perfect. I wanted them to be honest and heartfelt before anything else.

I am just a normal girl in her twenties, who likes writing about love and everything else that comes along with it. The good and the bad, the beautiful and the ugly.

Because, love doesn't need to be complete to be beautiful, and doesn't need to end happily ever after for it to be memorable.

I hope, that when you read this, you can remember the one you love. I hope you can relate to my words when I talk about falling in love as well as enduring heartbreak. I hope you can smile reading through my lines and realize that love is always worth pursuing no matter what.

Acknowledgement

Thanks to my amazing friend Autumn for helping me design the stunning cover and for always encouraging me to keep writing. I am honored to have an online friend like you.

Please follow her on Twitter - @AutumnK2022. She writes amazing romance stories and much more and currently is working on an 8-book series!

I'm eternally grateful to the wonderful writing community on Twitter, which gave me the confidence to write another book. Your support means the world.

Also, a very special thanks to every reader who finds and reads this book. Thanks for supporting my dream and loving my poems. I hope you find comfort in my words, just as I do in your encouragement and love.

1

Society Norms

Society Norms
They say we should follow

It's the only way to be happy
To find a loving forever of your own

People tell me
Fall in love and marry a nice guy

Have his babies; that's all you will need
That's the only way a woman can be happy

Don't fall for her
That's against everything right

You will never find happiness this way
That's what they say each and every day

But looking at her

ONLY YOU

I don't care about those threats

Perhaps loving her isn't what I should do
But happiness never comes without pain

I won't be accepted
Maybe we will never find a happy ending

As long as I get to love her from afar
I don't think I mind "the punishment."

Follow the rules
Do as we say; we know more than you

They tell me to listen to my mind first
But my heart is now too loud to ignore

All of your rules
What if I no longer want to follow them?

All I ever wanted was to love her more
Even if it is not the right way to live

Society norms
Perhaps we were never meant to fit

I don't mind crossing boundaries for her
As long as she is waiting on the other side,

I'll leave this behind
The society that keeps me away from her.

SOCIETY NORMS

Leaving her was never an option, anyway
I would rather be known as the rebel forever.

Introduction

Let me introduce you to my world
It has revolved around her for years

She doesn't know the truth yet
Tells me to find someone new too

With no words to say, I simply smile.
My love for her is evident in my eyes

Not yet ready to tell her what she means
I hide behind the shadows and love her

At times, I feel guilty about being ignorant
I keep hoping one day; I can tell her the truth

Maybe one day, I'll be brave enough to speak
And she will forgive me for all my mistakes

The future is far away and impossible to read

INTRODUCTION

So, for now, I will keep hiding behind words

Till then, my truth is in these written verses.
Louder than it has ever been, I'm sure of that.

3

One Sided Feelings

One-sided feelings
That's what the world calls my love

Saying it's never gonna work
And heartbreak is all I'll ever get

They ask if it's worth the pain
To love someone who doesn't know

Does the heartbreak not destroy me?
If her smile is enough to make me happy

Each time, I only smile in response
Never finding the right words to explain it

I can't explain how much she means to me
How she heals my soul without any words

If she loved me, I would have the world

ONE SIDED FEELINGS

But she doesn't know, and that's okay too

All I ever want is to have her beside me
Even if she could only be a dear friend

It's been years since the day we met
Years since I fell in love with her madly

Yet it all still feels like yesterday
That's how I know she's the one for me

4

Dirty Little Secrets

Buried deep inside these pockets
I think that's where you should be

Hidden from the rest of the world
Like many of my dirty little secrets,

I drew your portrait on the canvas
Colored it red like our broken love

Then I pretend you mean nothing
So I wouldn't have to talk about us

Right in front of you, I speak to others
Pretend that I care, but I really don't

It's just a fake picture. I want you to see
So behind closed doors, I can love you

Your love has taken charge of my soul

DIRTY LITTLE SECRETS

Even so, I continue to ignore my heart

I'm afraid you will find out my secret
So, I chose to distance myself from you

As days passed, my feelings have grown
There is nothing else that matters now

Lost in your eyes, I continue to fall more
Still, I'll never be ready to say I love you

I don't want to ruin what we have made
Don't wanna give you a reason to leave

So I convince my heart to move ahead
Still, I manage to see you in every crowd

My broken heart will bear your name
I promise to adore you forever, my love

But, it's only a friendship in your eyes
And maybe, that's the best thing for me

I wish we were more than we are now
I wish I was allowed to kiss you sweetly

For now, I'll hide you safely in my heart
So I can continue to hold you close forever

5

Unspoken Confessions

Words threaten to spill out
Halting at the corners of my mouth

Turning into a smile full of secrets
Another day when you are unaware

If only words were enough to tell
The yearning in my heart and soul

Scars of the past left bruises on me
Changing the honest truth into lies

I see the questions in your eyes
Yet the answer never escapes my lips

Perhaps I am too terrified to ruin
A beautiful world that you've given me

I promised to never keep any secrets

UNSPOKEN CONFESSIONS

But these growing feelings terrify me

Every evening, I lie awake alone
Suffocated by the secrets I've kept

A million unspoken confessions
Would you hate me if you know?

Scared, yet I wrote about my love
Hoping one day, words will be enough

Looking at you, I try to become brave
So one day to tell you all that I never said

Unspoken confessions weigh me down
All I am hoping is to say them out loud

For now, I hope these verses can speak
Telling you how much you mean to me

6

Almost

I try to think this way; you're almost mine
I am allowed to be with you, but can't stay

I can smile at you but can't kiss you yet
You don't know any of my hidden feelings

I hope things will get better between us
But the word 'almost' continues to ruin us

I don't want almost; I wish to have it all
A future with you that no one can take away

Each time we're okay, something goes wrong
Each time you promise to stay but walk away

I almost call out your name but then stay quiet
We say we're okay and yet continue to suffer

'Almost' is all that we seem to have now

ALMOST

How do we manage to keep losing each time?

I know we're meant to be, but you're not here
What can I do to alter the ending bound to come?

Past two in the morning, I think about us
Almost is the word that keeps me awake now

I want to ask what you think about that word
Maybe you detest it more than I claim to do

I can't accept 'almost' no matter how much I try
I wonder if you stay up at night doing the same.

Why am I not allowed to love you as I want?
Why can't I erase this awful word from our life?

I am tired of fighting, tired of accepting defeat
I want to make it to forever with you beside me

All we have is tonight; tomorrow is not ours
Let me kiss you, and hope forever can be ours

I know you want to love me, yet you walk away
As if you were never mine to keep and adore

Forget the word almost; I just want to love you
I only want to live if I can make you smile more

7

These Selfish Needs of Mine

These selfish needs of mine
I know they suffocate you

I wish I could change now
I wish I could let you be you

Sometimes I get infuriated
When you're busy with others,

I can't have all your time. I know
Yet I can't help but feel neglected

I know you love me just as much
But comfort is my drug of choice

I want you to be here forever
Don't want others in-between

You need time to be on your own

THESE SELFISH NEEDS OF MINE

To see your friends, do stuff alone

But each time you go, I am in pain
Never know when I'll see you again

I know I am too selfish at times
I know I ask for too much from you

Never give you enough in return
But I want to have you to myself

Trust me, I want to change too
Want to let you live life as you wish

But sometimes it's too much for me
All I want is to take you away with me

My love makes me selfish. I know
Shouldn't be this way, my heart knows

But never do I change, I hate it so much
Keep hurting you even without knowing

I am not the only one in your world
I need to be okay with that now, too

But my selfish heart, it never listens
Bitter inside, it continues to complain

You are allowed to be mad and leave
You can tell me to leave you alone too

ONLY YOU

These are nothing but my selfish needs
I know I shouldn't treat you this way

I love you, yet keep suffocating you
So push me away, I won't mind it

Maybe that's the only way I'll learn
To hide my selfish needs once more

8

Nothing but a Stranger

Tell me, where have you been recently
I haven't seen you in such a long time

You seem to message me every minute
Yet it's as if we haven't talked in a while

Don't know your routine or your secrets
I don't know the people you often meet

I can't recall when we last spoke normally
Maybe because we've drifted away lately

I haven't lost interest, but I am so tired
How do I tell you things have changed?

Perhaps you know, but don't talk about it
So we can avoid the possible heartache

You know about me through social posts

ONLY YOU

But it's difficult for me to know about you

I try to ask; the conversation ends quick
As if we both don't have much to convey

Perhaps you see why we are different
There seems to be a distance between us

I have loved you the same for many years
Then why can't I find what we misplaced?

The space won't let me sleep these days
When I think of you, I wonder what to do

Tell me what I can do to fix the mistakes
Is there a way we can get out of this mess?

I've been missing you, how do I tell you?
Whatever I do, the screen remains empty.

So I continue to miss you every evening
Hoping we can erase this distance soon

9

Some Days

Some days, when the silence stretches for hours
I recall the last time we spoke without a problem

I remember a time when love used to be so easy
I unintentionally sink into the depths of my bed

Some days, I don't know how to explain things
I don't want to talk about things that torture me

Some days, we have nothing left to talk about
So we both stare at the empty screen for hours

I force myself to find random topics to discuss
The conversation between us has become scarce

Some days, it's hard to keep what we have going
When we're a little too tired to address our issues,

I know we don't want to give up on what we have

But how can we repair this? I continue to wonder.

Some days, all we need to do is pause for a moment
Perhaps taking a small step back is not that wrong

Some days, it's okay not to speak if we are exhausted
What we have here is special enough to last a lifetime

So if you want to forget these issues once in a while
I swear not to blame you for being selfish anymore

Some days are harder than the ones we had before
Days that test our resolve to make things work

You might doubt your own power on those hard days
I might blame myself for things out of my own control

Some days, when things seem a bit difficult to handle,
Please remember the value of our love for each other

Maybe then we won't have to work hard to heal
So we can return to rebuild what we need the most

10

Insignificant Words

You always wanted me to speak more
You said talking would amend things

I lacked the courage to attempt to talk
We became even more silent as a result

Maybe talking would have helped us heal
Then perhaps you would have stayed longer

My silence gave you a reason to doubt us
I couldn't make you trust that I loved you

Tell me, are words really that significant?
My silence seems to hurt you more and more

I wish my actions were enough to tell you
That you are the one I treasure the most

I tried so much to let you know how I feel

ONLY YOU

My eyes followed you without much effort

As if you were the only one who mattered
That is enough to confirm that I love you

The world makes no sense to me anymore
Without you, I don't know how to be happy

Your absence makes it impossible to breathe
I never know how to convey my true feelings

If words are vital, I'd like to learn to speak
Maybe that way, I can make you love me

Baby, I want to give you everything you need
Even if you don't want me, I want to be here

Tell me what you need, and I can change
I will tell you all my secrets if you ask me

This distance between us is starting to hurt
Tell me what I can do to make you understand

Telling you my secrets maybe won't be as hard
But I don't know how I'll live if you're gone

Words have always been insignificant to me
But if I can keep you, I'll learn to talk more

11

Oblivious

Oblivious most days
I hate to see you this way

Ignoring me, knowing that I care
Sometimes it seems you do it for fun

Intentionally, as if you hurt me
Wanting to see how much I can take

You have always been this way; I know.
It still hurts the same when you fail to see

You know I've loved you the same, always
You made your choice so quickly still

As if you never cared to understand
The version of me that fell madly in love

Perhaps you see it all, all my pain

ONLY YOU

Don't know how to deal with the strain

So you ignore this, and we continue
Hurt me once, hurt me two times more

Or are you really that oblivious?
Too busy to see my pain-filled eyes

Heartbreak clear in my voice, as always
But you walk past as if nothing matters

You know, people came to tell me
How I am left to fight battles alone

Yet I wish you would be here once
Could see the reasons behind my silence

I love you the way you always are
I hope you can do the same for me

Wish I was strong enough as my real self
And not the one the world always hated

Tell me what to do; I am so afraid.
You know I have never loved this way

Heartbreak is not something new to me
But this time around, I am not ready for it

Never been so tired of the heartache
Maybe that's why I want you to change

OBLIVIOUS

The other side is where I have always been
All you have to do is come back this way

I'll let you be oblivious
But I am tired of giving explanations

Maybe someday we'll figure out the truth
Till then, let's continue the pretense game

12

Patterns

There seems to be a pattern
To the years we've been through,

For I always notice we do similar things
We get hurt and hurt others the same way

I don't think you mean all those words
Cruel complaints and hurtful sentences

They hurt nonetheless; I want to say
And in return, I do the same anyway

Love is not always enough. We both know
Sometimes the hurt seeps through the gaps

And so we hurt each other to make a point
To make the other understand all our aches

We cross boundaries between good and bad

PATTERNS

We know it's wrong, yet we commit the crime

Hurting ones we love, we hurt in return
We still continue, hoping to prove a point

These patterns, I know, you want to break too
I wish to change things, yet fear what will be

We keep repeating the painful pattern
Still hoping for a difference each time

I love you so much. I hope you still know that
Just because this hurts, we don't need to quit

I know love is worth it; we need to fight more
To break the pattern, to find the forever we crave

I notice all your patterns; never say a thing
I am sure you see mine and keep quiet too

What else can we do than ignore and move on?
Not always can we fix the problems we've spun.

Sometimes, a solution does not even exist
Bitter as we are, so we continue the patterns

An ache in our chest, we don't know the reason
We chase without knowing, so we continue to fall

13

Kiss Me Forever

Kiss me forever, I wish you could kiss me forever
Until my lips are bruised and all your doubts vanish

I don't know how to fix things so let's not think now
For now, just hold me closer so I don't come undone

We might come to an end soon, I know we are broken
But kiss me once more and I would ignore all this

I would kiss you back as desperately as our first time
I would make you love me if it was just for a moment

I don't want to talk, don't want to say things to hurt
I don't want to think about the times we both loathe

Just for a moment, let me forget how we messed up
Let's pretend we could still construct forever together

Kiss me a little more. I am too tired to argue more

KISS ME FOREVER

I know you want to end us, but I am not ready yet

Yeah, I am desperate, but how could I let you go easily?
I have never known a life where you weren't beside me

We shared many laughs and made memories together
I've learned to love you more than anything else in life

The end is near, yet I want to hang on for a bit longer
Kiss me again until we both forget our painful present

I know you are scared just as I am to leave this behind
So let us experience this beautiful feeling for a bit more

We can then recall a time when love wasn't as tough
We might discover a way to heal and move past this

I'm sure you can remember when our love was worth it
You must recollect, we promised to battle for our future

You want forever just as desperately as I do, I know
Let us hope that there is something still between us

Kiss me forever, that is the only way I could stay, okay
Broken beyond repair, you are the only one I want now

I want to hug you tonight and hope you stay tomorrow
Hopefully, then we'll be convinced to kiss forever

14

Someone New

I smile and listen every time you speak
With a permanent loving look and smile

I watched you fall in love with him, then
Helpless, too scared to tell you the truth

I was naive, not ready to fight for you
Kept hurting you, to hide my feelings

I thought I was making the right choice
Waking away to give you guys some space

I broke your heart; then he did the same
But not before you shattered mine to pieces

There's a chance you'll never love me
Yet I can't help but keep falling in love

I remember the first night you told me

SOMEONE NEW

About the new person you found to love

Broken, yet I told you I was happy for you
I had never spoken a bigger lie in my life

Whether you decide to stay or walk away,
I vowed to love you as I had done for years

So started the most brutal battle of my life
Smiling as you fell in love with someone new

15

Fight for Me Now

I am tired of chasing after you without a break
For once, I hope you were trying to fix this mess

I wonder if you quit caring about us a while ago
Maybe you were too good at showing pretense

I keep taking your side and saying you are busy
I keep telling others that you are trying your best

I see when they giggle as soon as I turn around
They knew I was too blind to notice your flaws

I wonder if you believe I am worth fighting for
If you know, I will give you anything you need

I don't mind being hurt if you get to smile more
But you don't seem to care about my happiness

For once, I hope you can come and see me first

FIGHT FOR ME NOW

Tell me that you want to protect what we have

Would you care if I left without a goodbye?
Or would you continue to live happily later?

Though never perfect, we had good moments
So many things about you make me want to live

I cannot help but fall in love with you each day
I keep wondering if you ever loved me the same.

Some days I see you and think you want me too
There are days when you want to hold me close

The fire burns in your eyes when you look at me
Those are the only times I think you need me

But then I see you live a life without troubles
Even if we don't speak, you seem not to care

Those are the moments I feel the weakest
Times that make me question if you loved me

I am going to take a step back; I'm exhausted.
For once, I want to wait till you come to me

Fight for me now. Let me see you struggle
I want to see you fight for my affection now

16

Leave Me Behind

You can leave me behind. I won't mind
If that is what you need to feel okay

Even if my heart breaks, I'll let you leave
You have to be content even if I'm hurting

If you want to walk away, don't hesitate
I need you, but I won't get in your way

Do whatever you want to find happiness
If you don't love me now, don't pretend

I know that you are tired, so I won't talk
Don't regret anything if you need to go

I know that you love me but cannot stay
It's okay, darling; maybe I'll be okay soon

I am not trying to make you regret

LEAVE ME BEHIND

I don't want you to hate what you want

The pain in your eyes breaks my heart
Choose yourself so I can breathe again

We have tried for years to stay together
You wanted to fix me, but I am too broken

Some things aren't meant to be repaired
So walk away now as I try to move ahead

Maybe someday, I will be in front of you
Better than now; perhaps then I'll love you

Yet if you find someone else, I won't mind
You deserve to be happy, even without me

I want to apologize to you; I won't now
I know apologies cannot repair everything

I will adore you more but say my goodbye
Hoping that one day our paths cross again,

I want to curse myself for destroying you
But I won't do that now. I know you hate it

I might be in pain, but you need to be okay
That way, one day, I will find happiness

Leave me behind, darling. I won't be angry
It's okay now; you deserve to be happy

Maybe right now, we are not meant to work
The future might let me adore you correctly

17

Reminisce

Sometimes, I wonder if you can recall the days
Sunshine all around, when we were both happy

We used to walk on cloud nine every day
Nothing wrong could ruin what we built then

I remember the days when we smiled together
I once used to be the reason you were cheerful

A small conversation with you was all I needed
To forget my messed-up reality once in a while

Since then, it seems as if a lifetime has passed
Now we are here, incapable of talking properly

Still hopeless, yet I have become more awkward
Somehow, we have drifted apart too much now

When silence rings for far too long, I think of you

ONLY YOU

I remember the days when we could talk endlessly

I don't know why time has changed us radically
We are now nothing but strangers without love

My only getaway is to reflect on the past years
I spend time trying to repair everything ruined

I want to return to when love was simpler
Possibly then we could learn to love once more

I want to ask if you ever reminisce like me
About days when we thought we were okay,

Maybe you know that there is an issue
Probably you are frantic to repair this today

Once in a while, I become hopeful looking at you
I have a small hope that we can make things right

When I remember those times, I fall for you again
I hope we can have those days back once more

18

Distance

See you over there
Standing alone

Wanna reach out
But no, I won't

I love you so much
But I'm hurting too

So I'll let you be
I'll continue alone

Listen to music
I am doing it too

Wish I could join
But I know I won't

I miss you so much

ONLY YOU

No idea how to talk

Love is in the air
But you are not here

But I manage to smile
Life goes on as always

Are you smiling now?
Or the pain is too much?

You must be hurting
Trust me, I am too

But nothing we can do
Except move forward

Tomorrow will be better
At least I am hoping it is

Till then, we should walk
Even if it's difficult now

So let me be alone
I'll let you walk away

Distance might be okay
Maybe it will do us well

19

Everything and Nothing

Love
It means everything and nothing

That's how I felt
The day I fell for you the first time

The entire world
As if it was all mine back then

Yet out of touch
I had to stay far away for years

Saw me at my worse
You thought I never cared

Saw me at my best
And you believed in the future

How could it be?

ONLY YOU

That we had it all at one point

Then lost in the battle
And now we wander searching

Yet the hope stays alive;
Every time I see you, I feel it

For love is never simple
But it makes life beautiful

And so I'll wait for it
The future that I once craved

Tell me when it ends
That's the day I'll have all I need

Till then I will stay here
Waiting for everything and nothing

20

Only You

I have been in love many times before.
I had my heart broken repeatedly.

Something about you keeps me falling.
As if you are the one I have waited for.

The time I recall being happy was here.
Beside you under the sky years before

Now I walk the same streets in fear.
Trying to learn why we're so destroyed

Return to me; give me another chance.
We can repair this and fall in love again.

Otherwise, I don't know how to live my life.
I can't fall in love with anyone except you.

We can recover the loss forever, I swear.

ONLY YOU

With just a little more time and care

I know we can make this work someday.
I can picture you with me in the future.

I don't know why you are the one I love.
I don't know what about you feels right.

It's something I lack that I see in your smile.
Maybe that's why you're the one I love.

You've seen my best; you've seen my worst.
You've seen me smile and shout as well.

From our youth until now, as proper adults
How can I stop loving you after all this time?

The place where I make sense is beside you.
Please tell me how I can walk away from this.

When my heart wants nothing else but you
When my mind has vowed, I'll only love you.

Till the end of forever, you will be the one.
The one I love even as time moves on

You are the one I need; would you mind?
I want to stay with you; you seem like home.

I don't know why, but my eyes only see you.
As if I can be happy only with you here.

ONLY YOU

Please don't ask me anything; let me stay here.
If you break my heart, let me still adore you.

21

An Obsession

People say love brings out the worst
You scream and shout just to be heard

Heartbreak follows anywhere you go
You can never escape the pain altogether

Looking at you, I know it's an obsession
Loving you comes with terrible consequences

Yet I never want to stop this crazy madness
I never want to walk away, even if it hurts

Perhaps I am at my worst. I am aware now
Screaming and shouting just to let you know

Without regrets, I've continued to fall more
Without fears, I allow myself to be vulnerable

Love is madness. I know we both believe that

AN OBSESSION

I won't be mad if you never understand me

My obsession, I know it has gone out of hands
But I don't know how to stop, become better

Rather be mental than fit into the normal
You know I'll rather be sad than happy alone

I should learn my lesson, yet I never grow up
Want me to change, but insanity is the solution

22

The Beach

I visit our favorite beach so often
Each day, I wish you were there

It has been months since we visited
I walk alone to relive those memories

The ocean greets me with a smile
Though I haven't smiled back in weeks

I try not to let him see the sadness
He knows everything without me talking

The ocean hears me talk about you
That is the only time I manage a smile

Those days are like a distant dream
As if the beach never saw us together

I cannot stop the tears that escape

THE BEACH

The ocean never judges my silent cries

Maybe the beach misses your presence
The waves howl more each time I visit

In the silence, I hear the ocean speak
Perhaps he also wishes to talk to you

I want to go with you once more
I am not sure it will happen again

Those songs we used to listen to there
Those stories that we shared back then

I recall and cry helplessly each time
Although those days are long gone by

Yet I go to the beach, hoping to return
To the place that was my home before

You're not here, so it always feels lonely
Without you, the beach continues to weep

23

All I Think

If anyone ever asked me what I think about
Perhaps your name is the only thing I'll say

I don't recall the last thing I had in mind
Besides the smile, you gave me back then

The entire world can't hold my attention
Your memories know how to distract me

Your name is all I need to forget everything
Then stay awake the whole night with a grin

I try to live my life as normally as I can
Make it through a routine I don't adore

Yet like a robot, I smile and laugh every day
Thinking about the last words you said to me

I still wonder if you think about me each night

ALL I THINK

Do my memories keep you away from things?

Do you struggle to focus on things around you?
Just because my thoughts don't leave you alone

I wrote all these words, thinking about you
The way you used to talk and how you smiled

I remember the last few days we spent together
The last time I was so genuinely happy was then

Are you still hurt? Again, I have made a mistake.
Not sure how to tell you I have damaged more

Now the negative ideas try to drown me again
Your memories are keeping me rational though

I haven't even gathered the courage to speak
I don't know how to say sorry to you this time

You are tired, so how do I tell my mind?
I desire to reassure you, but I don't know-how

All I can do is think about you as time passes
Think about you so I don't do something worse

I want to pause more so you can return to me
I want you to notice I'm still thinking about you

24

Fixable

A few feet away, you sleep peacefully
Yet the battles in my head resume again

I remember how I felt when you found me
Broken, desperately wanting to fix our love,

You told me it's fixable, and I believed you
Like always, your words comforted my heart

Now in the silence, I worry about the future
Thinking if we can ever repair all we've ruined

Even through the issues, I loved you the same
You had your doubts but loved me back as well

Still, issues remain; there's a lot more to say
We haven't forgotten the hurtful words we said

But I never stopped loving you. I know that much

FIXABLE

Never let go of the forever we dreamt of together

And so now, as we lay here, tired of all the fights
I know we can make it as long as we both try

Our future is blurrier, and I know you're scared
Trust me when I say I feel the same way too

But I hope you believe your own words still
I hope you know we can fix this together

Keep believing in our love; that's all I ask for
As long as you're here, I will keep trying more

And one day, when our future is our present,
I promise all this will be worth it to you as well

25

Trust Issues

Trust issues, you and I both got those
Yet we dive deep in, despite the fears

You know I fear the consequences too
Fear the heartbreak that is sure to come

I know you have got your doubts
Believing nothing ever lasts forever

Yet what can we do but give in again
Love, we both know it's all about risks

Who's going to stop us? I won't be the one
Trust me when I say I don't run from failure

Trust issues, they are sure to follow us
Haunt the present, make us fear the future

For me, the results were never important

TRUST ISSUES

You never said it's worth all the trouble

I want to show you; love is worth all the pain
But not sure if I even believe those words

All we could do was ignore our insecurities
Not let the anxiety stop us from falling in love

You don't need to trust me if you love me
I'll erase your trust issues if you erase mine

Look into my eyes, and I hope you can see
All my worries reflect the ones in your eyes

Trust issues, I hope you see I have them too
Be assured and take one more chance on us

26

One Word at a Time

I was not always this brave.
Someone who believed in happiness

But using one word at a time
You showed me the world could be good.

And that there's a place for me
And that people are willing to love me

When I look into your honest eyes,
I allow myself to try just once more.

With no real trust in my strengths,
But complete belief in the way you loved me

Now, many years have passed since then
I look at you and still smile with ease

There are no lies in your words

ONE WORD AT A TIME

I believe what you say so easily

Maybe I am not the bravest person
But your love gives me the power to fight

Once upon a time, I was broken too
Never thought I would live a better life

You never made any promises to me
But your gentle words showed me hope

And for the sake of our better future,
I live despite my insecurities and woes

One day, I know we hope we can make it
As long as you continue to be my savior,

Like the very first night, we met.
You stand beside me with the same smile.

And now, I smile back in return.
Trusting the future, you think we deserve

Because with you in my little corner,
I know I can conquer the hardest battles.

One word at a time, I am hoping
You heal me without knowing anything.

And I will still keep expecting
Continuing this way until we get better.

27

Mere Words

I wish mere words could explain to you
The way you make my soul feel lately

But words have never helped me
To show you how much I adore you

I have known you for so many years
Your tiny habits engraved in my mind

Those are the reasons why I am alive
Reasons why I can't stop falling for you

I've tried so hard to tell you how I feel
I've written so many confessions now

If you ever find my diary and read this
You might finally know my true desires

In my dreams, we have kissed for years

MERE WORDS

You have been mine for the world to see

But the reality is different; it tortures me
You aren't mine and can't stay beside me

So I turn to poems, hoping that they help
Maybe through words, I can speak my heart

I want to tell the world how amazing you are
How you manage to brighten my dark world

I am not a good poet, but I want to write
About every pretty crinkle in your eyes

I am not perfect, but you make me believe
That I deserved to be adored by you, too

Words used to come quickly to me before
Now they betray me when I write for you

As if no term in the dictionary is enough
Nothing can clarify how you make me feel

I want to keep trying, so allow me to write
Till the moment I figure out how to reveal

How perfect you are so the world can hear
The one I adored was nothing but an angel

28

The Future of My Dreams

I imagine a future far better than what we have
Each night on my pillow, that's how I fall asleep

Thinking about you is all I need to be okay
Even though our lives are far from perfect

The darkness of the past still looms over me
But your eyes show me the road to a home

Though there are times when I doubt my abilities,
It's easy to relax when you smile at me so prettily

The future might not be perfect, but it will be better
With you beside me, I think I can make it there too

I've never had someone who cared enough to stay
But when I look at you, it feels like you'll stay awhile

You have seen worse than me, yet you offer comfort

THE FUTURE OF MY DREAMS

Sometimes I look at you, and you seem like a dream

As if you don't care about the responsibilities on us
As you trust, we'll have the future we both desire

The future is unknown, and it keeps me up at night
It is possible tomorrow; we may have to walk away

But for now, I don't want to think about those times
All I need right now is for you to look at me lovingly

Hold me back, darling; I am falling too fast, easily
Stop looking at me as if you feel the same about me

The way you make it seem is a little terrifying to me
As if the future is ours, we just need to hold on tightly

I am almost convinced your smile can heal my soul
It reassures my soul without requiring much effort

I see a future with you, but it may be too much to ask
However, I can't help but want you by my side forever

29

A Little Broken

Before you decide to stay, I want to tell you
I am a little broken. Perhaps you can see it

Be a little gentle is all I can ask you now
Know that I have been a bit tired for a while

The scars on my body I can conceal quickly
But sometimes, the pain is visible in my eyes

You might be shocked to hear all my secrets
Those that I have kept hidden for many years

I may seem to be perfect, but I am far from it
Unavoidable problems continuously burden me

It gets hard to breathe with all the guilt I have
I can't even remember the last time I laughed

I don't smile a lot or talk about my emotions

A LITTLE BROKEN

You don't see me complain about my worries

There are days when I refuse to talk for hours
Times when it's hard for you to stay beside me

I know that it's not easy to be around me now
The way I am, I don't think anyone can love me

My broken heart still desires for you to stay
I'm broken, yet I wonder if you will be with me

There's so much that I want to explain but can't
Don't lose your patience as I try to mend myself

It's getting difficult to fake, so please let me cry
Perhaps then some of my wounds can be fixed

If you trust me, maybe I can repair everything
A little strength I hope you can offer me now

I know that this battle is entirely mine to fight
Still, I wish for someone to have my back as well

I am a little broken, however; I do hope you stay
I want to love you as much as you have loved me

Just keep smiling at me; my soul is healing slowly
Maybe then, one day, it won't be as broken as now

30

Be Here Tonight

Hold on to my hands tonight; I am a little scared
About the unknown future and all that is to come

I don't want to close my eyes, don't want to dream
About a beautiful day just to wake up on my own

I used to live a nightmare, one that never ended
Now that I have seen this, I don't want to return to it

Whisper in the dark tonight to soothe my tired soul
For I have been on this journey for too long, I'll say

Let's pretend a bit more till this haze settles down
For tomorrow may not be as beautiful as tonight

No one to disappoint, so I smile a little more today
But maybe tomorrow, the dark clouds will take over

I seem to have forgotten the good times you recall

But they only hide the ugly truth that we live lately

So I hope you hold me tight tonight; I am not ready.
To face the world that I left behind head-on just yet

Be here tonight, so I can pretend things are the same
We may be able to walk away tomorrow smiling, then

31

Teach Me to Dream

Teach me to dream
I haven't closed my eyes in a while

Get me to stand up
I haven't seen the world in some time

Please remind me to breathe
For I have been struggling for weeks

Tell me it's alright now
Since I have blamed myself too much

Ask me to try harder
I haven't had a purpose in life

Maybe I'll find something
That makes life beautiful once more

You've seen me sad for days.

TEACH ME TO DREAM

Perhaps you are wondering how to help

A little more than love, it takes
To fix something so broken inside

Ask me to hold on some more
For my grip has been slipping for a while

I don't know what it will take
But maybe it's that sweet smile you gave

No solution in sight, yet we try
Every day I wake up to find a new purpose

Maybe one day, I will find a reason to live
As long as you are there to remind me to try

32

Walk Into My Dreams

Stroll into my dreams tonight
Perhaps that's how we may meet

Away from this cursed reality, too
Then maybe we'll both smile again.

Do whisper in my ears tonight.
The secrets you've kept for years

So I could tell you all of mine too
And we could both finally be free

Do give me all your false excuses
Let me pretend that I am okay too

So we could forget this past of ours
And reach for a non-existing future

Do tell me of all the things you lost

WALK INTO MY DREAMS

So I could offer some false comfort

As if the world hasn't tired me out
Just like how it tired you out before

Do come again to tempt my senses
Make me fall in love once more now

Perhaps I can pretend you never left
As if you never broke your promises

Do think about me one last time, love
Think about the times we smiled here

Perhaps then I can hope you'll return
To restore everything we've ruined

Do stroll into my dreams tonight
Cause I am too tired to stay awake

Maybe then you will see my regret
And learn I never stopped loving you

33

Those Moments

Roaring over my wild heart
Faster than the passing trains

The sound of your voice comes
To bring another batch of smiles

It's been a while since we first met
Been a minute since I fell for you

Yet seeing you again feels the same
As if I still could fall all over again

Gentler than the wind in my hair
Are your words as we speak quietly

You remind me to breathe like before
Ground me just before I could collapse

Surprised to see you still beside me

THOSE MOMENTS

Yet grateful I get to love you a bit more

Prettier than these evening scenes
Mesmerized by you, I watch you more

As if the pain never destroyed me
As if I have more to learn about you

Those rare moments of happiness
Sometimes I forget all about them

But in the loneliest moments of life
They are all that keep me a bit sane

Bad memories rush away from us
Faster than these vanishing stations

As if they don't hold power over me
As long as I can continue to love you

34

Beautiful Disaster

Falling for you was like waiting for a disaster.
A beautiful disaster I would never regret facing

Your crystal eyes dared me to walk towards the edge.
Mine asked if you would be able to take the same risk.
Doomed from the beginning, yet I chose to love you.
Hold you close, and your million scars even closer.

I handed you my heart, which had already been damaged.
Knowing that you would destroy it more than anyone else
Endless regrets in my heart, but loving you isn't one.
I wonder if life would be better if I never fell for you.

But one look at you, and the pain seems worth it.
To see you smile, I will accept death with open hands.
There are days when you hesitate to take my hand.
Moments when I struggle to believe you also love me

Still, I manage to move towards you without any fear.

BEAUTIFUL DISASTER

I doubt myself, yet I never manage to doubt our love.
What a beautiful disaster life has been since I met you.
No moment of happiness has ever stayed long enough.

We have made many mistakes, yet somehow you are here.
I wait for you to regret this, but I never see you walking out.
Would you call it a disaster even if we are better now?
Though the road hasn't been easy, we've managed to stay

I don't know the future or when the past will return.
All I know is that I am falling for you more in the present.
Even if this is a disaster, it's more beautiful than anything else.
Broken in every corner, yet somehow we manage to shine.

I won't promise you forever; we are still learning to believe it
But remember, I want to stand beside you in case we ever find it.

35

If I Fall For Someone Else

Maybe I will fall in love with someone again
I don't know the future, so I can't promise

But one thing I know for sure, I can promise
I will never love someone as I have loved you

Some other gorgeous eyes might distract me
Yet the shine in yours I will never forget

I might smile if I see some beautiful smiles
Yours is the only one I will keep in my heart

The next time I am in love, I might be happy
Yet it won't compare to what you have done

The way you have changed my life so much
No one else would make me feel that amazing

You know I value anyone that I ever find here

IF I FALL FOR SOMEONE ELSE

But something about you seems so different

Possibly, my heart will find someone one day
I swear it will continue to search for you

I don't think anyone would equal your smile
The way that you effortlessly make me okay

Yes, I might eventually find the right person
But you will always be my soulmate, my love

How can someone else take your place now?
When you are the one who taught me love

I don't think I've ever fallen as I fell for you
Tell me, how can anyone be better than you?

I've never been this sure about anything else
Even though the future ahead is still unclear,

even if I fall for someone else in the future
Even so, I promise you will never be replaced

One day you might discover that I cherish you
When I'm already in love with someone else,

But still our memories, I vow I won't forget
I promise I won't fall for anyone else this way

36

Even if I Don't Remember

Even if a day comes when I don't remember
My own name or the purpose of my silly life

I know I'll recall the way you used to giggle
Over the stupidest jokes I once used to tell

Even if a day comes when I don't remember
Everything that once meant the world to me

I know I'll recall that I have loved you forever
You are the one I wish I never cease to recall

Even if a day comes when I don't remember
The small things that used to make me happy

I know I'll recall how easily you made me fall
As if you were always meant to own my heart

Even if a day comes when I don't remember

EVEN IF I DON'T REMEMBER

Writing all these poems or who they are for

I know I'll recall the ones I wrote about you
Days when, for some reason, we couldn't talk

Even if a day comes when I don't remember
Everything I vowed to remember forever once

I'll recall the first time we stood under the rain
We have a friendship that I'll always treasure

Even if a day comes when I don't remember
Details that have blurred over the past years

Even then, I'll remember your weirdest words
For those are the reasons I fell in love with you

Even if a day comes when I don't recollect
My own identity or the reasons why I am here

Even the day when we no longer talk regularly
I will remember you, and I know that for sure

37

One Day I Won't Walk Away

One day I won't walk away
A day when our home will be the same

You know, a day like that is far away
But I promise, one day, it's going to come

Through this struggle, I continue to walk
Believe in the future; that's all I've done

Even when the past chains me to grief,
You know I'll try for our happiness

Each night, you know I dream the same
Each day, I wake up hoping for the same

Days when nothing ever makes sense
You know I look forward to when it will

A reason, perhaps I don't have a good one

ONE DAY I WON'T WALK AWAY

Maybe not all is fair in war and love

I've never followed the rules as I should
I'll never play fair when it comes to you and I

My eyes follow you; you know they hope
For a change and still, hang on to the rope

I've never dreamed of a luxurious life
I'll find a home anywhere I could have you

Out in the world, I won't be restricted
One day, I'll live the life of my dreams

Make your choice. You know I won't feel hurt
Remember, I'll always hope for you to stay

One day, I promise never to walk away
From a home I wanted to have with you

One day when I have the choice of my own,
I'll always choose you without any doubt

38

Safe and Sound

Love should be safe and sound
At least that's what people said

I looked for comfort for so long
I ended up finding it in your eyes

You ask me if I've ever been in love
If I know how it feels to be obsessed

I look at you and smile in response
Never knowing why you are the one

Terrified, I walked these roads alone
Looking for a savior, looking for hope

You found me on the day I had given up
It made me believe life can be beautiful

Safety is elusive; at least, I feel that way

SAFE AND SOUND

Never have I been able to sleep peacefully

Still, I picture your perfect smile each night
Lately, it's the only thing keeping me afloat

Maybe that's why it's easy to fall in love
Even when the consequence is no good

A punishment indeed, to fall in love with you
Yet nothing can make me stay away from you

Used to being the savior before you came
I pulled the hero card and tried to fix things

But with you, I allow myself to be weak
And somehow, I have found my happiness

Perhaps that's why I love you. I am not sure
Safe and sound, nowhere but beside you

I smile despite the pain each time I see you
Wishing for you to save me from hell again

Nothing more I could do but offer my love
So I could try to relieve some of your pain

I hope I give you some happiness in return
Safe and sound; I hope that's how you feel

39

Beautiful Stranger

A beautiful stranger was all you meant
In front of my eyes, with a pretty smile

With a nervous grin, I listened to you talk
With nothing to say, I stayed mesmerized

Now years later, we still stand here
Across from you, I try to make sense

The world that we live in, isn't very kind
Yet you make me want to believe in love

A couple of times, my heart was broken
The time that felt like it would never pass

But you make me want to do it again
Give love another chance; I hope it works

Maybe you don't feel the same

BEAUTIFUL STRANGER

Perhaps another heartbreak is all I'll get

Walking these streets together is a bliss
And it makes me wish for forever more

I didn't know your name or anything else
The sparkle in your eyes was all I needed

Miles away from the day we first met
Now we continue to fight for a future

I've never trusted any other person
But I give you it all without hesitation

Will you also break my heart? Maybe
Your love has always been worth it all

I gave you all I had the day we first met
Without knowing what the future held

Making you mine never was my goal
But it's all I dream about every night

Beautiful stranger, I met you in darkness
Your light leads me toward happiness

The road is long, with more heartbreak
Yet I'll walk towards you with a smile

40

Always hers

She walked into my life like a stunning dream
As if she was meant to be mine from the start

But her eyes always focused on something else
Something that never was the love in my eyes

Yet with every smile, she grabbed my attention
With every word, she made me hers effortlessly

Until there was no part of me that existed alone
I felt alive only when she was smiling by my side

Falling in love with her was the happiest change
One that never scared me as I held on to her more

She tightened her grip on me as more time passed
Until I could no longer fight the love I had for her

But then she walked away without explanations

ALWAYS HERS

As if she never owed me anything to say goodbye

And that was true, for this was always one-sided
As her love for someone else continued to bloom,

Now she is with me, yet she has never been this far
She dreams about a love that she never got to have

Beside her, I smile and watch her love someone new
Once again, like before, with someone who isn't me

She never played fair, but I won't accuse her, anyway
I was the one who kept my heart concealed forever

So I could sidestep the hurt that may destroy me
for when the time comes, we have to walk away

She walked into my life like a captivating dream
I refuse to think how it would be without her

Because life is amazing even if she doesn't know
That my heart has been hers to keep and to break

41

Home

I've been running for ages
Without a goal, with no end in sight
Without a home, nowhere for me to belong

No place like home, people said
But my own never seemed comfortable
So I looked around the world for another one

Then one day, I found it in your smile
In your eyes, in your promises of tomorrow
In your words that made me believe in love

Who was I before you? I can't remember
All I can recall are the moments spent with you
Perhaps because that's the happiest I've ever been

With you, I am on top of the world
My soul and my heart, now all belong to you
I am nothing else but a worshiper of your love

HOME

If a home is really where the heart is
You are my home, there is no doubt about that
Nowhere I would rather be than with you forever

My home, it's not a physical place
Not a house made of bricks and four walls
It's in your heart, where I wish to live forever

42

The Month of December

It was the month of December. I still remember
The first time I admitted I was in love once again,

Christmas lights around me, yet I couldn't focus
On anything else but your lovely smile that night

Snow blanketed the streets, so people went home
Sat around the fireplace as they smiled together

But the fire ignited in my heart for the first time
Trying to warn me that I was about to fall deeper,

As the season changed, my feelings changed too
No longer could I pretend that you meant nothing

Whenever I looked at you, I could see my fondness
Feelings I had buried were impossible to hide then

We spent hours together walking random streets

THE MONTH OF DECEMBER

My heart fluttered as you giggled at my silly jokes

The more I watched you, the more I fell in love
I didn't want to fall in love, but I couldn't avoid it

A part of me feared you might hurt my feelings
I was aware you might leave me behind one day

However, there was something about that winter
I couldn't help but crave your warmth since then

I've known you forever, but new feelings took over
Each time you hugged me, my heart thudded loud

The most agonizing part was saying goodbye to you
As though my heart knew you would disappear soon

After December had ended, I still couldn't forget you
By the time summer approached you were long gone

However, a part of me hoped you'd come in December
So I waited for winter, hoping it would bring you along

I'm still deeply in love as another December comes
This year, I'm not sure if you will join me for a stroll

Yet, I smile as the world is again covered with snow
I recollect the December when I fell in love with you

Also by Mia Sanchez

If you liked this book, please check out my first poetry collection "Symphony of Secrets". It is available as an e-book and paperback all around the world.

Symphony of Secrets
***"The image you had of me was inaccurate;
The absence of the symphony of my secrets
made it a completely distinct story."***

When I started writing this poetry collection, that was the first thing that came to mind. Maybe it was because I never thought anyone would understand me.

All of us have fallen in love and had our hearts broken. Over the years, we have lost friendships and felt lost at least once. In those moments, you just want to find something that would help you express your emotions. Poems for such moments are included in this collection.

No matter what your situation or where you are, hopefully, you can find at least one poem in this collection that speaks to you.

www.ingramcontent.com/pod-product-compliance
Lightning Source LLC
LaVergne TN
LVHW041619070526
838199LV00052B/3202